Aviator

Aviator

Poetry by Richard Chandler

ISBN: 9798599842019

Layout by Rachel Greene for elfinpen designs, http://elfinpen.com

Cover by Amelia Greene.

Introduction

This collection includes many poems that were not part of my previous volume, *Water From the Moon*, as well as several written subsequently. The earliest poems have been recently revised, as they seemed virtually unreadable in the original, even those that were published back then. One of these, 'The Mermaid on the Reef', received an award over 30 years ago—and writing this now, I suddenly feel very old…

One may notice a good any sonnets in this volume, as there were in its predecessor—well, I can explain that…! Clearly I've always loved sonnets, and when a writer works in a certain form for some time—35 years, let's say!—he or she starts tending to think in that form. The sonnet is endlessly useful in framing topics and positing questions, has a very illustrious history, and overlays a certain order over the language that free verse, for all its excellent qualities, by design does not do—besides, I've always loved sonnets.

This collection also reflects some of the trauma of the awful year 2020, which brought a pandemic to the world, along with an economic and political crisis to America. We will come out stronger and wiser from the dilemmas of that year, and our culture is certain to not just prevail, but flourish after these challenges. This book was completed very near the close of the dystopian year 2020, in part in answer to it.

Several of these poems had been published in magazines and journals between 1990 and 2010, including in *Manna*, *Thresholds*, and *American Poetry Journal*.

Aviator

The Dancing Cranes

Let love take a bow
And all sorrows will go,
Their dark reports discarded—
All of their heart-falls
Are only thin vignettes,
And never meant to last.

There are dancing cranes
Who shudder white, like snowfall
By ices on the lake—
The winter descends around them,
And they just shake it off.

We know you feel discarded,
And that counterfeit love
Can hurt worse than curses;
But forgive yourself—
The lessons won't be kept,
And love will dance for you.

Romantics

Sunsets are only turnings of the planet,
Magicians only have tricks up their sleeves;
The pyramids are only so much granite,
And pirates on land are just common thieves—
Without romance the commonplace is sterile,
As mathematics must look to a bird;
We lose our sense of wonder at our peril,
That serenade that isn't often heard.
You say you're never one to be romantic—
But there's a flash of mischief in your eyes
That's never so dismissive, nor pedantic
To never catch the edges of surprise.
It's never just a random happenstance
That love's still in the service of romance.

Richard Chandler

Another Day on the Moon

This place has no atmosphere.
Look around, and all you see
Is gray on gray, day after day;
Any date you name, more of the same—
The cold, the stillness, the black sky,
Day for night, and nowhere to go
When up above's just like below.

No storms, no clouds, no botany—
Just a whole lot of monotony;
Sooner or later you'll come to a crater,
And when something drops in
It hits like a meteor.
Those who left footprints
Haven't been back since,
And there's no telling midnight from noon—
It's another day on the moon.

She's Still the Same

She's still the same, while all of us grow older,

As though her portrait—well, you know the line;

She's warmer where the rest of us grow colder,

Sidestepping nature's relentless design

That's tapping so insistent on the shoulder,

The way that leads us all into decay;

It isn't just the eye of the beholder—

She's changeless as the sunrise, day by day.

We courted when the pyramids were younger,

Andromeda less distant than today,

When love was more immediate than hunger—

Ignore what the clocks and calendars say,

Timepieces chiming off days on a tone—

Love runs on a timetable all its own.

Richard Chandler

All Flowers Could Be Gray

All flowers could be gray—or the same shape,
Pheromones alone calling insects in—
Tress could be a uniform size and shade,
And all liquids dry as mercury.
We could all look the same, like sand fleas,
Only knowing our kin via something within.

Something in nature gives us extras
That sets the arrays in splendid displays,
That silks the diaphanous;
There must be a purpose to the April flourish—
For the spectacle of nebulae
Where there's nobody to see them.

Mystery Play

This isn't another Agatha Christie,
And there are no subtle clues to be found;
The isn't a moor gone foggy and misty,
Nor are there tracks of a phosphorous hound—
The author's not another Raymond Chandler,
Is not another Edgar Allan Poe—
But subterfuge can hide itself in candor,
And we can be deceived by what we know.
This is a mystery play that we're seeing—
Personifications, a moral bent,
And all wrapped up in the great chain of being;
If all that's below has been Heaven sent,
And every birth's christened with an angel's kiss,
There ought to be no mystery in this.

Richard Chandler

Carnival

Is it raining where you are,
As it has been in here?
There's a mist in the distance,
And the hills are silver-blue,
Where flocks of heron make their way
Down the white and quiet sky—
Yesterday, beings of papier-mache
Were busy parading by.

And those of us who stay nocturnal
Recorded everything in a journal—
Swallowers of swords, of fire;
Assistants on the spinning-wheel
Where the blindfolded throw knives,
And the Vegas bookmakers lay odds
On who survives.

If you're contented, then all is well—
Music plays for the holidays,
And colors twirl at the carnival
To the snaps of castanets;
Someone's ringing bells in the courtyard,
And strangers raise glasses up in song
To the pitch of a penny whistle.

What Is Love?

Love—what the hell *is* it? Is it illusion,
The something exquisite that Sappho sought?
Is it a madness that leads to seclusion,
Or is it best defined, by what it's not?
We've all been there, we've all been
                              on the carpet,
The cross-hairs of the telescopic sight—
Whether you're the shooter, or the target,
Whether you've come to pardon, or indict.
Love plays the same old shell game
                              through the ages,
Then changes shapes, and soon escapes the net—
The poets write innumerable pages,
And still there's no convincing likeness yet.
Love is nobody's fool, and not the kind
To stay still long enough to be defined.

                                          Richard Chandler

A Loyal Friend

A loyal friend is like the Northern Star
For mariners on an uneasy sea—
A compass telling here, and who you are,
Even to pointing where you need to be;
While other constellations come and go,
That star is beacon to the heaven-bound
Who rise above the carnage here below,
Where other wayward ships have run aground.
If you're deserving of a loyal friend
Who knows you well, and loves you just the same,
Who doesn't check the ledger at the end,
Who's waiting even when you come up lame;
One of the last to leave, and first to help—
You're probably a loyal friend, yourself.

Aviator

Amelia walks out from her dream,
And the wreck of the Electra;
She misses her maps and her flight plans,
The comfort of her compass—
The island's little stone idols
Regard her with a hectic silence;
She almost made it—
She's more famous now, missing.

Was she the Emperor's guest?
Had she banked her too far west,
And into the South Pacific?
We've found no navigational charts,
No skeletons, no airplane parts—
Nothing certain, nothing specific.

She was the pioneer—
The High Priestess of pilots,
Buzzing the atolls and islets;
Now, one rickety recording
Of "running north and south".
Barnstormers are dropping leaflets
From Guam to Nikumaroro
That read, "Amelia will fly"—
The next leap of faith, is hers.

                                                    Richard Chandler

Spring Tanka

In cherry season,
Winds chequered white with petals—
Cranes fly overhead.

Over the mirroring lake,
Thoughts are blown and scattered.

The spring sun sets
In a bed of green and yellow,
Near the lemon fields;

On the wind, the sound of bells
Echo from a closed window.

The late rain's glazing
Shimmers along thin willows—
I remember you.

We were together so briefly,
When you were called away.

The evening music
Might just as well be silence,
When you are not here.

Beside the April stars,
The city lights are pale.

Did I hear your your step
On the rounded wood porches?
—Intruding sparrow.

Richard Chandler

For Tawny

She made an art of living in the present,
Yet always kept remembrance of the past;
She knew that life wouldn't always be pleasant,
But understood discomforts wouldn't last;
She'd run to catch the first sunbeams of morning,
The dawn light tawny, and the tree tips red;
Every day would be a day worth exploring—
Emotion on four feet, as someone said.
Sleepy and stretched in the evening's patina,
She might have dreamt of treasures hid away,
Or running in the sand by the marina,
Joyful in the tidal line, and the spray—
Now every day's fidelity and play,
Yesterday no different than today.

Time Piece

The next second always beckoned,
The promise of something rising up
Among the fertile and the fecund—
Everyone's waiting for the witching hour
With conical hats, and comical noses;
All spirits, wanting to be blithe.
That's Time all right, wielding a scythe.

Tomorrow is like a magician—
Flowers in sleeves, rodents in hats,
Assistants out of position;
Another illusion to botch,
That everyone stopped to watch.
And the future is a one-way mirror—
Stand there and stare as long as you like,
The image won't get any clearer.

Richard Chandler

If I Were You

If I were you, I'd wonder at this writer
Who tosses all these sonnets in my way—
Wearing uniqueness like a bishop's miter,
Insisting art's as common as the clay;
If I were you, I'd question that ambition
That sets to conquer what's already won,
Mistaking opposition for sedition,
And leaves the least accomplishment undone.
You'd understand why there might be elation
Attending any random thought of you—
And even if the train has left the station,
And the next done the line is overdue,
You'd see how love, unruly as the sea,
Could calm with you in mind, if you were me.

High Summer

They say a star danced the day you were born—
Astronomers would know if this was true,
And whose who map ascensions of the morn,
Dealing in futures, like the mystics do;
They say you were born in a merry hour—
Likely true, though they say your mother cried;
And were that day the only day to flower,
The ensuing bloom would be the world's pride.
It's right your birthday doesn't fall in April,
In competition with the blooms in spring—
The purple irises, the season's staple,
The scarlet roses, first in everything;
Nor is the fall or winter right for you—
Only the glories of summer will do.

Richard Chandler

Sif's Saga

The moon above Asgard tonight
Shines likes a diamond on the fjord—
The dim light sparkles on the white lanes,
On the high walls of frost and ice
That circle round the citadel
Of castles surrounded by clouds;
Odin is quiet on his high throne,
And Sif, she of the raven-black hair,
Considers her return to the world.

Nothing's the same as they left it,
When the days were wrapped in wonder—
Nobody fear Loki anymore,
And now the thunder's only thunder.
Do gods fade away without worship?
Do the rune stones speak anymore?
Down here the ravens still caw at dusk,
The amber-reds still edge the dawn,
And the twilight is so soon gone.

Firewalker

You said you never cared for poetry,

That versifiers must be up to something—

You're not the only one of my coterie

Who'd only take this bet double or nothing,

Who see the imposition of a sonnet

The way astronomers might foresee

An immanent collision with a comet,

And that opinion isn't lost on me—

But as this summer circles lines of fire

Along the helpless ash trees and the pines,

Even the devastation will inspire,

Even the broken walls and fallen lines

Will speak, and the blackened, cindered wire

Will testify of those who play with fire.

Richard Chandler

Nightingale

Is a nightingale singing on the palace grounds?
We've searched the ringed gardens and the walks,
The quadrangle courtyard and the ivied walls,
And we've seen nothing—the only other sounds,
The whirring wheels and the ponderous clocks
Re-echo and chime the interdicting time,
The day-in, day-out that tells us nothing.

Is a nightingale perched in this vast domain?
The works and days that take the soul to task
Will never listen to a plaintive refrain,
Of nature erring from itself— no la me so la,
A future nurtured in the comforting straw,
The native wood notes of some natural law.

A nightingale sings of the temporal—
He knows the darkness is only nocturnal,
His dark is not the darkness of the emperor;
Tonight's only sound is the sleepless owl,
And under the floorboards and stones, a shifting—
The future uncoiling, beginning to growl.

Endurance

It's not as though I miss you every day—
Although I miss you oftener than not,
And insecurities I'd kept at bay
Close in with the celerity of thought;
And though I seldom write you when I might,
Or wait for things to right before I call,
It only means the minions of the night
Are closer than the ghosts who haunt the hall.
But when you stay away from me too long,
Then every day's a question of endurance—
It's as if all the universe is wrong,
And I'd give anything for reassurance
That all is as it was, before you came;
You come, you go—and, everything's the same.

Richard Chandler

A Word From You

Letters arrive from loved ones,
Some who don't know I exist—
They guessed at my address, and missed;
Some from those I hardly knew,
And still, not a word from you.

Some people grow tentative, wary
Of sharing what they choose to carry,
And some just aren't epistolary—

But while my writing's hardly gold,
More like waves on the wavy sea,
I'm fine with missives COD.—
I'm fine with postage due;
The Ephesians' claim to fame is,
They were written to.

And the past is ashes in an urn,
The days fly by and never return—
And still, not a word from you.

Missing You

I miss you only when the sun is risen,
Or when the moon is somewhere in the sky—
The feeling cuts like a careless incision,
And lingers like the winter trailing by;
Since you're so far away, time unrolls slowly,
In opposition to its native bent—
Eventually, the evening sun sinks lowly,
And no accounting for where the day went.
Did we fall short? Did we cut ties too soon?
Did we miss a step, or simply stop believing?
Were we deluded, thinking we're immune,
And did we catch it just as we were leaving?
Once we were closer, or, that's what I thought;
I could have been mistaken—we were not.

Richard Chandler

Lucky Seven

Seven's never a lucky number,
When it's people in the billions—
There's too many groups of wallflowers,
Too many hoops at the cotillions.
Even in the coffin you don't feel alone,
And you mop three brows, before your own.

Increase the surplus population,
And add to the evils we choose—
Who's finding rice for everyone,
Who's cobbling together the shoes?
There's another child born
Every 40 seconds—
And tomorrow, another day beckons.

The Magicians

I never write so well as when you're with me—
It sounds good, even if it isn't true;
The verses sound fine, the dialogue's pithy,
And nothing I write is true about you.
I never dreamed so soundly, so profoundly
As when the dreaming brings you close as this;
Creation so astounding all around me,
Whenever you are close enough to kiss—
But once I wake, and once I start to focus,
I see deception's crept up and moved in;
Perceptions altered, as though by a lotus,
And any mitigation's wearing thin,
If ever there—magicians never share
How a ball *seems* to hover in mid-air.

                                                      Richard Chandler

These— And Yet, Not These

It was in subtle looks, unread books,
And sentences one word could derail
That left our love on tender hooks—
It was in the unexpected pauses,
Sleepless nights, bar fights in saloons;

It was in these— and yet, not these
That I lost touch with you.
We gamble so much on just one toss,
We risk it all on a single call
And never account for the loss.

I still hear you in the ringing bells—
I feel your touch on each heirloom
I've tucked away in my spare room,
And see you in the russet sunsets
Where swallows ascend over stones
That wall the towns beside the seas;
It's in these—and yet, not these.

I'd Do Anything For You

You know I'd do anything for you, don't you?
The phrase supposes endless possibilities,
And once I've claimed there's nothing I won't do,
The whole idea makes me ill at ease—
If I could guess why happiness eludes us,
Address deficiencies, and stop up gaps,
I'd know what in the best of love precludes us,
Why every effort ended in collapse.
You know I'd do anything for you, don't you—
And once I've made this extravagant claim,
I wonder if I've ever really known you,
And I suspect you might just do the same,
Which makes my statement rickety, at best;
Yet I'll still stand by it—or near, if pressed.

Richard Chandler

Reconciliation

If you and I should ever reconcile,
We'll let the champagne freely flow all evening—
And as it's said in Shakespeare's play, we'll smile,
And lie about which one first thought of leaving;
We'll edit every memory with style,
Forgetting how we tinged our world with grieving,
But missed out on forgiveness by a mile,
With no-one taken in by our deceiving.
We'd spent too many weekends on the fence,
Our afternoons all coffee spoons and silence—
And kept too many clues in confidence,
Slipping of the edge of our alliance,
Deceit and supposition and denial
Our underpinnings, while we reconcile.

This is Not a Sonnet

It's obvious that this is not a sonnet—
Or if it was, whatever else it is
That carries all these implications on it;
A sonnet's not supposed to break like this,
Its lattice of support about to shatter;
Annihilating, if used the wrong way,
As if it were composed of antimatter—
A moment here, then subject to decay.
This won't be curative to someone broken,
Nor will it justify God's ways to men,
Nor lead eternal truths out in the open—
Such sentiments are useful only when
Times are in turmoil, but surely passe
In the calm tranquility of today.

Richard Chandler

Gymnast

She edged onto greatness
Whenever she stepped up,
Her name echoing the arena—

Then she's the center of attention,
And the air of expectation's so thick,
No knife could cut it;

Then, she'd fly—high over the bars,
Vaulting, somersaulting, to land
With her hands raised to heaven.

And she floated like a dream
Over the four-inch beam,
Head high, eyes wide, legs straight…

She *was* great.
What inspired her to sacrifice so much,
For such a limited run?

And what must inspire her now,
With her triumphs denied,
Her dazzling career cut short;

And, why? Nothing she'd done,
That ended with a quirk of fate—

Was it perfection that chased her,
Eating the stretch before her,

And the timer always ticking,

Always at her, like a curse,
Just before she took a chance
On every leap, every landing;

A smile, a triumphant pose—
Then, flowers offered at the close.

Richard Chandler

You're My Everything

Why you're my everything, I cannot tell—
But after all this time, I feel the same;
You've made mistakes—I've made a few, as well,
And if I'm brokenhearted, I'm to blame.
You come before all others, that is true—
Though why I can't quite put my finger on,
It seems I'm more myself when I'm with you,
And like a stranger's shadow, when you're gone.
When everything's careening off the rails
You're a still center, and a quiet light—
When even Zen and meditation fails,
You're still the quiet of an autumn night,
When the soft leaves shiver,

                      and the moon's high—
You're everything, and still I can't say why.

On the Pacific Coast

On the sea-line,
The surging blue starting-line,
Mollusks and leftover shells
Linger on the morning sand;
The ocean is restless, slightly swaying,
As though to a sea-song
Sounded in the cloudy depths.

There's some old white wood on the beach,
Pieces of tree, resembling bones
Of some dislocate colossus.
There's fragments here and there
Along a close infamous cove,
Where distressful ships once ended
In the smoky coastal fogs.

In the hush of night, when the moon is on,
There's a hundred lights on the hill—
Below, starfish, weeds, jellies and gulls
Wait to their turn for the maternal sea.
Starlight's slanting off green edges of the bluff,
The whitecaps come to call,
And the expatriate shells shine vividly,
While the ocean keeps her secrets.

Richard Chandler

The Mermaid on the Reef

Let others worry time away—
We played by night and danced by day,
And re-read old romantic lines
By candles and Italian wines.

But darker thoughts discarded those
Like whirlwinds over Alpine snows—
You offered once mid-April words,
And songs that might out-sing the birds;

We loved when love was not in play—
When strangers gave their hearts away
To gaudy styles and vain parades,
To thin and empty accolades.

We know that time won't always burn,
And from its path we won't return,
But we'll let others turn that leaf—
We've seen the mermaid on the reef,

The scattered petals on the slope,
The Persian sultan's standing rope;
The magic lovers understand,
When everywhere is wonderland.

Doppelganger

It's as if you were a total stranger,

As though you could no longer trust us;

Not you at all—maybe, your doppelganger,

Wary, suspicious, even when it's just us.

You led me to the center of a circle

That spins its satellites into its star—

And as each evening's blue slips to purple,

I can't quite tell which one of you, you are.

It *couldn't* be you—it must be your double

Who has this tendency to shoot on sight,

Who searches the incendiary rubble

For maybe one more spark that might ignite—

And even if I called you out on this,

I wouldn't know which one of you this is.

                                   Richard Chandler

Arion's Lyric

The singer went overboard
Into the changing elements,
And vanished under the whitecaps;
On the surface, the rippled silhouettes of sailors
Waited for bubbles, or a surfacing.
On the billowed purple they found only a laurel,
And the silver edge of a lyre.

*Quad mare nescit Ariona tellus?**
A dolphin buoyed him over the waves,
And the poet sang such melodies
As steadied the sea, even to calming
The swift whirlwind, or so he says.
The dolphin carried the singer to shallows
Near his home in Taenaros,
Only for the magic of a song.

**From Ovid.*

If Only

If only you were not so far from me,
And lending your uniqueness elsewhere—
The dawns there should seem more spectral,
The lofty gardens more lively,
And sea-songs on the passing ships
All the more melodious;
Where I am, the days go by in shadow,
The monotony is odious,
And those paths I'm compelled to follow
Are rimmed with rust and empty faces.

If only you were here with me,
To render the time luxurious,
Far from the callous and commonplace,
The insistent, and the spurious;
We'd tease out the hidden mysteries,
Obscured, elusive and inconclusive,
To revel in beauties of the world
Like tiny figures in silkscreen paintings,
And dance along the verges of the sea—
If only you were once again with me.

Richard Chandler

Inspiration

You will always be the only inspiration
That conjures mythic figures in the sky,
And fires the forges of imagination
By just the merest glance or brief reply—
With every turning of the constellations
The present intermixes with the past,
And you will always buffet the relations
Between who comes in first, and follows last.
Your inspiration's the only gift given
To those who offer what's not theirs, to you;
And those who've known you will always be driven
To far excel the limits they once knew—
Often more so than any could explain,
Inspired like the equinoctial rain.

The New World Order

One belief for everyone—
One size fits all;
No temple bells, no nuns in cells,
No wailing wall.
There's no requests for visas
Where no-one keeps a border,
In the new world order.

One currency's good everywhere,
By land or by sea—
It's what the free market will bear,
And nothing is free.
Somebody here sets policy
In this shadowy polity—
One who rules like a warder
In this new world order.

Richard Chandler

Perpetual

Time's unending and uninterrupted motion
Stretches perpetually to the close
Of all existence, and this simple notion
Belies how little Mankind really knows
About the fabric of what's universal,
The slow unravel of eternity—
We bet the farm on gradual dispersal,
When all we found around here's uncertainty.
There's retreating on this headlong journey,
No traveling through Time, so we could meet
Those first explorers who departed early,
Opposing traffic on this one-way street—
Some think Time might curve, bend or reverse;
Some think that Time will end—

or, something worse.

Clairvoyance

Could someone really read your future,
Divine through a swirl of tea leaves
Or judge by the fall of the Tarot?
Summer narrows into autumn every year,
Every year green turns scarlet and gold—
It doesn't take a mystic teller to see
How the quick turns of time will unfold.

Gaze into this crystal ball, as they say,
And see that time shoots by like a laser—
Off like a light, and it's coming this way;
This interdiction's rife with predictions,
But the future may be written already,
However the balances steady.

Richard Chandler

Mistakes in Love

Mistakes in love can sometimes last forever—
Come howling when all other ghosts are through;
One roll of loaded dice, lean on a lever,
And the trap that's meant for others, catches you.
Too many liberties taken at leisure
Will leave the scatterings of what you've done—
All these supports that will bend under pressure,
The structure collapsing, once it's begun.
There are mistakes not subject to revision,
And not so readily explained away—
So much depends on a single decision,
A sudden bend, or the wrong word to say
At the wrong moment, and it all falls flat—
Mistakes in love are oftentimes like that.

Prayer to Aphrodite

Forgive me, Aphrodite, I have sinned—
It's been forever since my last confession;
Too often I've thrown caution to the wind,
Counted on equivocation, concession,
And gambled fortunes I did not possess,
Knowing the game was fixed from the beginning—
I wagered all I had, and nothing less,
And never had the slightest chance of winning.
I offer up oblations and a prayer
In hopes my many sins may be forgiven—
In your high holy temples everywhere,
In each romantic poem ever written.
If learning how to love should be my penance,
I won't petition for a lighter sentence.

                                                    Richard Chandler

Where Poetry Lies

Some say that poetry is born
In-between the pulse of ticks of seconds;
But we both know that isn't so—
Poetry's in the moment that beckons.

Some say that poetry is formed
Along the undersides of lightning;
But I tell you, that isn't true—
Poetry lies in the gold dawn's lighting.

Some say the poetry is warmed
By disdainful forgers in the skies;
But I still say, it's not that way—
Poetry's found in the beloved's eyes.

Approaching Autumn

Everything changes when beauty takes hold—
The greens that occupied the farthest grove
Now startle with rushes of blown leaves of gold,
And colors summer cradled with such love
Give way to orange and russet expanse,
Scattering patterns of yellow and red,
The tardy flowers joining in the dance,
And the cool winds whisper of autumn ahead.
And yet, as familiar as all this is,
The changing of each season of each year
Still thrills my heart with anticipating this,
As summer's coaxing slowly disappear;
A child's excitement at the light of dawn—
The slow approach of autumn coming on.

Richard Chandler

The Vampire

He looks like a pale shadow
Loosed from its natural twin;
Ice on claws, and hair on palms,
He rises like a mist, like a wolf—
Not only when the moon is high,
Not only when the moon is full.

Is he proof that the Devil exists—
Does he imply his counterpart?
What process sidesteps nature,
And allows a dead man to rise—
The tight-lipped smile, the lifeless eyes,
The fear of the rising light?

The shrouded stars of autumn
Shine like the beads of rosaries,
And words to ward off those like him
Sound in the prayers of votaries;
His past is one long dead end,
And his history, *is* history
(Though no reflection on him)—
But for all his potential harm,
He still must be invited in.

Spirits

Why would one spirit remain as a phantom,
When everyone else enters eternity?
Surely it isn't haphazard, not random,
Not an inquiry of such urgency.
What is it traces that curious vector
That so deflects the never-ending path,
That now and then a soul becomes a specter,
Unaccounted-for in life's aftermath?
Some came to blame a life's irresolution,
And some say violence creates a ghost—
Neither idea offers any solution
To one of those questions that matter most,
Why some are accepted, and some denied
Along the journey to the other side.

Richard Chandler

After the Nightmare

You're free again to walk the night air,
No matter what monsters had gone that way,
No matter what else once walked there unaware;

You'll be with those who comfort, and who care
For those who chose to stay, and come-what-may
Dismiss the lies, and torch the witch's lair.

The dominion of darkness can stop right there!
We can tell the Evil One—not today;
The morning breaks on celebrations everywhere.

Shadows

In sunlight our shadows walk together,
Mirroring our movements through the day,
Relying on vicissitudes of weather
And how the rays might bend or arc our way—
But in the evening, do the tricks of optics
Get restless in the surrounding dark,
To swap our secrets and resurrect topics,
Dividing the house, and dousing the spark?
If flint can start a fire, we're like our shadows,
As insubstantial, as soon here as gone—
Imperiled as a vessel in the shallows,
Dependent on the torchlight, or the dawn;
We're shadow-thin all the time we're here,
And when the darkness falls, we disappear.

Richard Chandler

Triceratops

She sees her world bordered by horns—
A world of rain-sparkled fronds
And small mammals under the cycads,
Vast grassy plains and high blue hills,
A sky of pale grays and varying reds.
The young huddle inside the spiral
Of strong adults, who keep watch
For any sudden movement.

This herd is in migration
To some warmer nest-place;
Nowhere is safe, but in some spots
The evening cold isn't so cutting.
Duckbills nearby, so water's close—
Old track ways of tyrannosaurs,
And everywhere, ruts of heavy tails.

Volcanoes plume in the distance,
Pterosaurs pop in and out of clouds;
She raises up her massive frill
To a pleasant scent, or it is for her—
She's secure in the pageant of her kind,
And for now, as cooler winds are rising,
She rests in the first of early flowers.

When Last We Met

I remember salmon plates and cognac
When last we met,
And brief divertimentos playing—
We spoke of Shelley and his circle;
You had to get back to your life,
A life you'd never shared with me.

Moonlight skirted the sea,
And the waves held the light.
We spoke about what wasn't then,
Never of what could have been—
I remember tinny bells
You only hear in season.

There were children waiting for you
When last we met,
Two of them, yours—brief words,
And a home to keep in tact;
Now, memories are fading thin—
Dissoluble, like aspirin.

Richard Chandler

Cold

God likes it cold.
The deepest sea is chilling,
The mountain summit's freezing,
And our space is nippy
Like you wouldn't believe—
For every hot sun and Sahara,
Every fire-rimmed caldera,
There's a million parsecs of icy,
Out where standing still is dicey.

God likes it empty,
For most of existence is
More nothing than something;
Even at the molecular level,
There's room to swing a cat—
Even in each stretch of space,
Is a stretch of empty space.

Winter Angels

Are there angels descending, circling, upending
Preconceptions that we're all alone?
Reckless and errant, gilded, transparent,
They'd spin along the contours of the globe,
And strafe the water lines, the freeway signs,
And arc in iridescent arabesques
In the visible air, if they were there.

Angels are spiraling, soaring and rivaling
The hummingbirds and the gliders,
Riding inside the swirling aurora,
Radiant while skipping off snow drops—
Their outstretched wings shimmer in flight,
Reflecting the midwinter night
The hopes for better times to come.
They'd glide the frozen trees and frosted walks,
And rest atop the close winter clouds
That hover everywhere, if they were there.

Richard Chandler

The First Snowfall

How magical—the first snow of the season!

What beauty fallen sudden on the air!

Emotion overtakes you beyond reason,

A misty hush descending everywhere,

And memories of long-forgotten wonder

Revive the child's instinctive rush to play,

The hopes that all-too-often knuckle under

To prioritizing, day after day.

Only the littlest change in temperature

Can bring you back to when life was a dream,

A moment's glimpse of when the world was pure,

And all you might believe in or redeem

Was in your reach, was at your beck-and-call,

Untouched and timeless as the first snowfall.

Christmas Present

You see a figure in the gilt and gaudy,

Cold and bony, with a skeletal hand—

And in among the tinseled and the tawdry

Is not the future anyone had planned;

And those of us who skirted through the dangers

That carried all the evils of the past,

Now look on our own shadows

                        like they're strangers,

And nothing that's eternal seems to last.

But now, in the ascendancy of solstice,

Someone leaves presents underneath a tree—

If not in joy, there's a measure of solace

In every searching journeyer we see,

And those who huddle under frosted eaves,

In the eerie stillness, the frozen leaves.

Richard Chandler

Christmas Eve

The holiday streetlights flash green and red,
The carolers keep time before they leave,
And even though mistletoe's overhead
I don't feel Christmas—and, it's Christmas Eve.
The indoor firs are shimmery with tinsel,
The icicles sparkle the boughs outside,
And seasonal songs from some passing minstrel
Sweep along the avenues like a tide;
And even as the evening frosts the holly,
The moonlight silvery in the night sky,
I ask why man can't overcome his folly—
Could ask all day, and I'll get no reply.
Even now, I don't know what to believe—
I don't feel Christmas, and it's Christmas Eve.

One Day

One day we'll understand the dolphins
When they speak, when they click and squeak,
And learn what secrets they'd impart

About the alien world under the waves,
And the baffling way that sea life behaves;

One day we'll know why galaxies revolve
Through endless quadrants of emptiness—
A mystery that's not so easy to solve.

Not every question merits a solution,
And often truth carries some disillusion,

But isn't it a gamble worth the risk,
To delve into the very root of things,
However often the scoffers tsk tsk?

The riddle's not all the curious solves—
One day, we'll better understand ourselves.

Richard Chandler

Celebration

A cause for celebration
Can be any old occasion,
Though some are better than others—

There's too much dissipation
Undermining where we stand,
And evil's always close at hand;

But we can outmaneuver this,
Vault over any obstacle
Once we've got a running start.

We join in on the joyful song
To the blue perimeters
Of this circumpolar sky,

And celebrate the rising light
That shines over flowering fields,
On the April flowers, the vying birds,

The dance that animates the day;
It skirts off the whitecaps,
And sparks like flashing cinders

In the fireplace of a hearth—
The sunrise cresting the hillside,
And the comfort of its warmth.

Richard Chandler

Dancing Cranes, 2020

You may see dancing cranes who high-step
Off the shoreline of the lake,
The strips where the elements mingle-
They tangle in the joy of living;
They ask nothing of the sun and sky
That's not already passing by.

There's too many dorsals outside the portals,
Intersessions, spurious lessons,
And missed long-distance calls—
In any strip of sediment,
You'll find an impediment,
And too many build on sodden ground;

But life reveals a kaleidoscope,
The same way light unpanels a prism—
The curious design of the wavy line
Circumventing nature's catechism.
The pulses pound in every sound—
Listen, and in the still soft hours,
You'll catch the cranes at dancing.

Thank You

I know no way to show my gratitude
For these surprising kindnesses you show,
Selfless as any I expect to know,
And offered in this humble attitude;
Any reply sounds more like a platitude,
And no-one in the rounds that come and go—
The angels above, the strangers below—
Could defend my response its lassitude;
Even so, though I never could repay
The gracious favor shown in all you do,
And while these spindly words are weak to say,
Few you hadn't heard before, and nothing new,
It's more than words I offer up today—
My thanks are poor indeed, but all for you.

Richard Chandler

Acknowledgments

I thank first and foremost my family for their endless support and patience—Rita Castillo, Cynthia Sinclair, and Robert Spencer—their belief in me has meant everything. I also thank my friends, old and new, who have proven so gracious and generous over the years; I thank God for Her watchful care, and of course my lucky stars, that I've come through this far.

Lightning Source UK Ltd.
Milton Keynes UK
UKHW022038140223
416982UK00010B/580